1864

Cities, towns, and railroads from Atlanta to Savannah, Georgia, are destroyed.

April 14, 1865

While attending Ford's Theatre, President Lincoln is shot by John Wilkes Booth; he dies the next day.

July 1-3, 1863

Battle of Gettysburg

November 8, 1864

Lincoln is elected president for second term.

January 1, 1863

Emancipation Proclamation is signed.

April 9, 1865

Confederate general Robert E. Lee surrenders to General Ulysses S. Grant at Appomattox. The Civil War ends.

Map of Major Civil War Battles

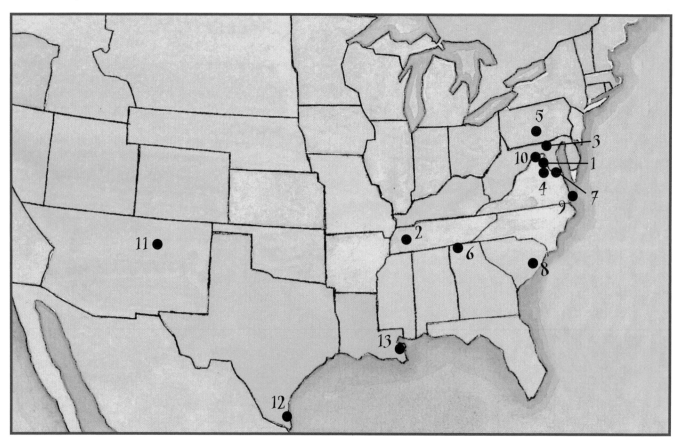

The battles of the Civil War were fought between April 12, 1861, and May 13, 1865. They resulted in the deaths of more than 620,000 Union and Confederate soldiers.

1	First and Second Battles of Bull Run	**7**	Battle of Chancellorsville
2	Battle of Shiloh	**8**	Battle of Fort Sumter
3	Battle of Antietam	**9**	Battle of *Monitor* and *Merrimack*
4	Battle of Fredericksburg	**10**	Battle of the Wilderness
5	Battle of Gettysburg	**11**	Battle of Glorieta Pass
6	Battle of Chickamauga	**12**	Battle of Brownsville
		13	Battle of New Orleans

Kid Pick!

Title: _____

Author: _____

Picked by: _____

_____

Why I love this book:

_____

_____

_____

Author:
Thomas Ratliff studied American History at
Central Connecticut State University and the
University of Connecticut. He has taught English
and history in middle and high schools, as well as
history and secondary education courses at college
level. He is also co-author of several young adult
historical novels set in the Civil War era.

Artist:
David Antram was born in Brighton, England,
in 1958. He studied at Eastbourne College of Art
and then worked in advertising for fifteen years
before becoming a full-time artist. He has
illustrated many children's nonfiction books.

Series Creator:
David Salariya was born in Dundee,
Scotland. He has illustrated a wide range of books
and has created and designed many new series for
publishers both in the UK and overseas. In 1989,
he established The Salariya Book Company. He
lives in Brighton with his wife, illustrator Shirley
Willis, and their son, Jonathan.

Editor:
Karen Barker Smith

Assistant Editor:
Michael Ford

© The Salariya Book Company Ltd MMXIII
No part of this publication may be reproduced in whole or in
part, or stored in a retrieval system, or transmitted in any form or
by any means, electronic, mechanical, photocopying, recording,
or otherwise, without written permission of the publisher. For
information regarding permission, write to the copyright holder.

Published in Great Britain in 2013 by
The Salariya Book Company Ltd
25 Marlborough Place, Brighton BN1 1UB

ISBN-13: 978-0-531-25947-4 (lib. bdg.)   978-0-531-24503-3 (pbk.)

All rights reserved.
Published in 2013 in the United States
by Franklin Watts
An imprint of Scholastic Inc.
Published simultaneously in Canada.

A CIP catalog record for this book is available
from the Library of Congress.

Printed and bound in China.
Printed on paper from sustainable sources.
1 2 3 4 5 6 7 8 9 10 R 22 21 20 19 18 17 16 15 14 13

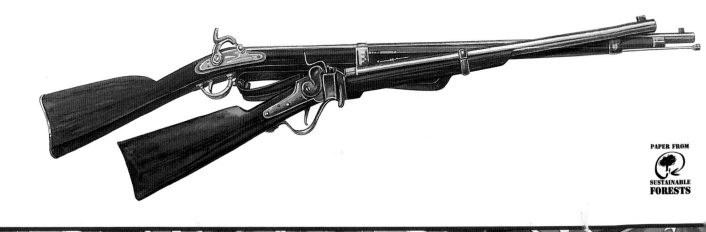

PAPER FROM
SUSTAINABLE
FORESTS

You Wouldn't Want to Be a Civil War Soldier!

Written by
Thomas Ratliff

Illustrated by
David Antram

Created and designed by
David Salariya

A War You'd Rather Not Fight

Franklin Watts®
An Imprint of Scholastic Inc.
NEW YORK • TORONTO • LONDON • AUCKLAND • SYDNEY
MEXICO CITY • NEW DELHI • HONG KONG
DANBURY, CONNECTICUT

Contents

Introduction

ou are a farmer living in a small town in Connecticut. After Abraham Lincoln is elected president in 1860, eleven southern states worried about the issue of slavery decide to secede—to leave the United States and form their own country, the Confederate States of America. Within a few months war breaks out. In the North, people want to preserve the Union and get the seceded states to return. In the South, most people want to preserve slavery and keep their new independence.

In the spring of 1861, President Lincoln calls for volunteers to sign up for 90-day enlistments in the army. You decide to serve your country and join the Union army. Everyone expects the war to be over in a few months, but in fact you will remain in the army for the next four years. In that time, over two million men will serve in the Union army, compared to about 700,000 for the Confederates. Casualties for both sides will total 620,000 deaths, making the conflict America's bloodiest war.

Hurrah for the Regiment!

You have enlisted in one of your state's infantry regiments. This means you will be serving with people from your home town and surrounding communities. The regiment has about 1,000 soldiers, divided into ten companies. You are one of 82 privates in Company K under Sergeant Wilson. Your regiment is part of the Army of the Potomac, stationed just outside Washington, D.C., the nation's capital. The army is supposed to protect Washington and threaten the Confederate capital at Richmond, Virginia, 100 miles (160 km) to the south. Opposing you is the Army of Northern Virginia, commanded by General Robert E. Lee. Throughout the war these two large armies will fight many terrible battles.

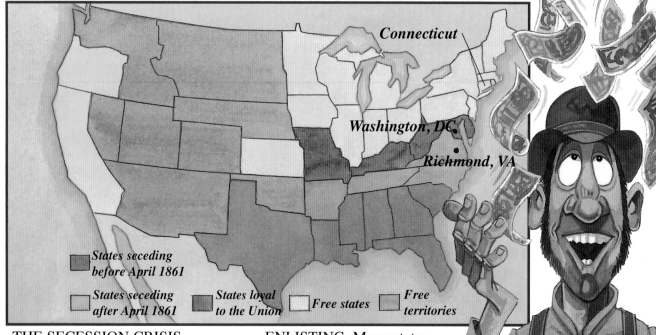

Connecticut

Washington, DC

Richmond, VA

States seceding before April 1861

States seceding after April 1861

States loyal to the Union

Free states

Free territories

THE SECESSION CRISIS. In 1861, slavery was legal in 15 of the 34 states, but four slave states, Delaware, Maryland, Kentucky, and Missouri did not secede. West Virginia, originally a part of Virginia, became a state in 1863.

ENLISTING. Many states, as well as cities and towns, offered bonuses for enlisting in the army. The bonuses could add up to several hundred dollars (far more than a year's basic soldier pay).

Union cavalry soldier

Handy Hint

If you are married, bring your wife along. Although most wives stayed at home, many women followed their husbands during the war. Married women often cooked meals, mended and washed clothes, and tended to the sick and wounded.

It'll be just like home—cooking, mending, washing—you'll love it Mildred.

I tell you, I don't want to go!

Union artillery soldier

Union infantry soldier

INFANTRY, ARTILLERY, AND CAVALRY. There are three kinds of military units: infantry, or foot soldiers; cavalry, who rode horses; and artillery, soldiers assigned to fire cannons. Like you, most soldiers in the Civil War fought in the infantry.

Cannonballs

What's Life Like in the Union Army?

Who's Who?

You can tell from the brass insignia on a soldier's cap whether they are in the infantry, cavalry, or artillery. Your cap has a bugle, which signifies the infantry.

Cavalry cap

Infantry cap

Artillery cap

Life in the army is very different from how it was on your farm. Everything you do is governed by regulations. All soldiers have to wear Union army uniforms, which are blue with brass buttons. You have a wool cap with a leather brim. The uniforms are wool, which keep you warm in winter, but they are hot and itchy in the summer. Food in the army is not as good as you are used to. Each week your company gets supplies—pork or salted beef, flour or hard bread (called "hardtack"), beans, peas, coffee, sugar, and salt—to feed all the men. Your company has a cook to prepare the meals, but regulations state that he has to boil the meat and vegetables for several hours, so the food is not very tasty.

Company cook

I'm boiling it for another three hours – it's company rules.

WATER. During battle you will get very thirsty. You can't just get up in the middle of a fight and go to look for water. Keep your canteen with you at all times!

Water canteen

Handy Hint

Even if you don't like the food, eat when you can. On a long march or in battle, the only food you can carry is hardtack, which makes your mouth very dry.

How about you do the washing and my **wife** does the cooking?

SALARY. A private in the Union army earns $12 a month. In the 1860s you can eat in a restaurant for 25 cents, mail a letter for three cents, and buy a suit of clothes for about $2. Most soldiers had some of their pay sent home to their families.

Will I Have My Own Bedroom?

Bedroll

Pack

Rifle

Canteen

nfortunately you will be spending most of the time outdoors. You share a small, two-man tent which is really two halves that button together. When you are marching, the tent is taken apart—you carry half the tent and your tent-mate carries the other. If you are marching long distances or fighting a battle, you won't have the time to set up your tent and will often just sleep on the ground. During the winter, there isn't much fighting. Many soldiers in your company build huts to live in and collect furniture to make life more comfortable. Some even have small stoves to keep warm. When the fighting starts up again in the spring, you have to throw out everything you cannot carry with you.

FULLY DRESSED. A soldier carries all of his gear in a pack, including clothes, dishes and silverware, personal items, and a bedroll. You also carry your canteen, rifle, bayonet, and cartridge box.

Summer

KEEPING CLEAN. If you want to take a bath, you will have to find a pond or river, which might be fun in the summertime, but is almost impossible in the winter. On marches or during battle, you won't have time to wash, comb your hair, brush your teeth, or change your clothes.

Winter

On long marches you can have some of your gear, like your tent and extra ammunition, carried in wagons. Since you may have to march several miles a day, the lighter your pack the better.

Handy Hint

That looks heavy.

Snore! snort...

SPARE TIME. You and your friends will have lots of time on your hands in the winter. To amuse themselves, the men in your company like to play baseball or dice, organize singing and storytelling groups, or write letters home. Mail from home is important since it keeps up morale.

The First Battle

A few miles south of Washington, D.C., is Manassas, Virginia, an important railroad junction—a key location for moving men and supplies. Union generals decide to capture the railroad and your unit is part of a large force that marches south toward Manassas. Confederate forces move north from Richmond and a battle is imminent. The fighting starts early in the morning. Deployed along a small creek called Bull Run, you don't really see the enemy, although you fire your weapon a few times when ordered to do so. The battle is mostly loud noises and smoke and it is hard to tell who is winning. At about 4 PM the Confederates receive reinforcements and you are ordered to retreat. The first battle has ended in defeat! You are hot, tired, and very thirsty, but you have to march all the way back to Washington, D.C., before you can rest.

SPECTATORS. Many people from Washington, D.C., came to observe the battle. They were dressed in their best clothes and some brought picnic lunches. The road to Washington, D.C., was clogged that evening by retreating soldiers and wagons filled with frightened civilians.

Another glass of ginger ale?

Was Life Different for a Confederate Soldier?

In the Confederate army, cavalry soldiers (right) have to supply their own horses. You have to be a very good horseman to ride in the cavalry.

During the Battle of Bull Run, your unit captured a few Confederate soldiers and you are ordered to guard them. You learn that the life of a Confederate soldier is not so different from your own. Their uniforms are grey wool, similar to yours, but not all Confederates have uniforms and some don't even have shoes! They have muskets instead of rifles, but many are excellent soldiers and the Confederate generals are experienced and skilled. The food in the Confederate army is not as good, or as plentiful, as you are used to and they have fewer doctors and nurses. But they are Americans, just like you. You realize that the Southern soldiers have to endure the same hardships you do: living outdoors, long marches in extreme heat or cold, loneliness and homesickness, and the dangers of battle. Throughout the war, soldiers from each side will often treat each other like friends and trade news, stories, and even goods like coffee and tobacco.

I hope you boys like hardtack and beans.

14

Confederate cavalry soldier

Handy Hint

Try not to get captured!
Even if prisoners of war were
treated well, many still died
of malnutrition, disease, or
from a lack of clean
drinking water.

What, no grits?

DIFFERENT
BACKGROUNDS.
Most Confederate
soldiers grew up on
farms and were used
to horses and guns.
Southerners expected
their soldiers to be
superior to Northern
soldiers, many of
whom were from
cities and had never
fired a gun before.

15

The Seesaw Battles of 1862

In the spring of 1862, your unit goes into action again, this time on the peninsula east of Richmond, Virginia. In a series of battles known as the Seven Days, the Union army is forced to retreat to Washington, D.C.. A few months later, General Lee launches an invasion of the North. Your unit marches for several days to catch up to the Confederates. The two armies meet in Sharpsburg, Maryland. Union troops, deployed along Antietam Creek, see plenty of action. The fighting is terrible and it seems that neither side is going to win. However, by nightfall you see that the Confederates are retreating. Your entire regiment lets out a loud cheer. Your first victory!

Victory at Antietam

That'll show 'em!

A BLOODY DAY. The joy of victory does not last long as you are assigned to help collect the dead and wounded (below). The Battle of Antietam—also known as the Battle of Sharpsburg—was the worst day of fighting in the entire war so far. There were over 12,000 casualties on both sides.

FREEDOM. After Antietam, President Lincoln issued the Emancipation Proclamation, which freed all the slaves in the Confederacy. During the war, over 179,000 African Americans served in the Union army.

Handy Hint

It is always better to defend a position than to attack. One reason for the high number of casualties at Antietam is that both sides were attacking in the open, with no defensive protection.

President Abraham Lincoln

"...I do order and declare that all persons held as slaves henceforward shall be free..."

I need a vacation.

The aftermath of Antietam

17

What Kind of Weapons Will I Use?

Union cavalry sword

CAVALRY SOLDIERS are equipped with swords and pistols. The sword comes in handy when there is hand-to-hand fighting.

Many Union weapons are made in your home state of Connecticut. Sharps rifles are popular since they can be loaded and fired faster than the older muskets. Colt Firearms produce revolvers which fire six shots without reloading. These are popular with cavalrymen, since it is difficult to reload while riding. You are proud to carry a modern Sharps rifle.

Many Southern soldiers still use more inaccurate muskets. To load a musket, the gunpowder and a lead ball are put into the muzzle. Then a small amount of powder is put in the priming pan. When the trigger is pulled, the hammer strikes the priming pan and gives off a small spark, igniting the powder and firing the musket.

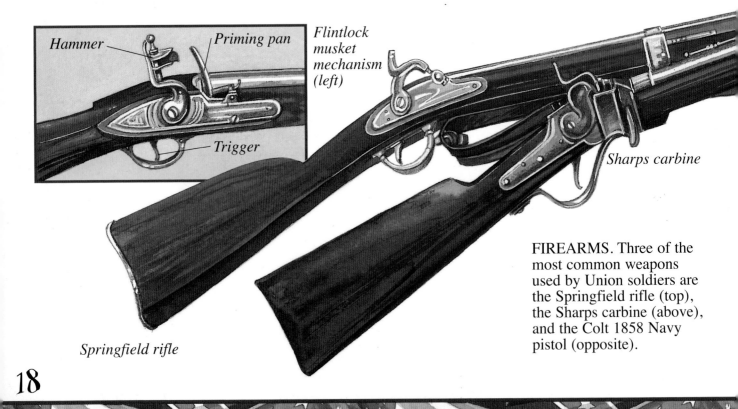

Hammer

Priming pan

Flintlock musket mechanism (left)

Trigger

Sharps carbine

Springfield rifle

FIREARMS. Three of the most common weapons used by Union soldiers are the Springfield rifle (top), the Sharps carbine (above), and the Colt 1858 Navy pistol (opposite).

Handy Hint

Your cartridge box holds about 40 cartridges for your Sharps rifle. Keep track of how many you fire. If you run out you might not be able to find more right away.

Colt Navy pistol

AN AMAZING VICTORY.
At Gettysburg, a Union unit from Maine ran out of ammunition while defending a position. However, they still managed to defeat an attacking Confederate regiment by charging into them and overwhelming the attackers in hand-to-hand combat.

Turning Points: Gettysburg and Vicksburg

General Robert E. Lee

In June 1863, Lee launches an invasion into Pennsylvania. The Army of the Potomac, now commanded by General Meade, moves quickly to meet the Confederates. On July 1, your unit runs into an enemy regiment just north of Gettysburg, Pennsylvania. The battle grows to a terrible scale. For three days, 85,000 Union troops are pitted against a Confederate army of 75,000. By the time the battle ends, over 50,000 men have been killed or wounded. Lee's army has been forced to retreat in what is the greatest Union victory yet.

PROBLEMS ON THE MARCH. Marching in the summer is unpleasant. It is hot, thirsty work and the dust is unbearable. To make matters worse, your wool uniform is so itchy you can hardly stand it.

On the same day, Confederate forces in Vicksburg, Mississippi, surrender the city to a Union army under General Ulysses S. Grant. Grant had laid siege to the city for several months and the surrender meant that the Union army controlled the Mississippi River. Five months after these battles, a national cemetery was dedicated at Gettysburg by President Lincoln.

General George Gordon Meade

Handy Hint

If you are wounded you might find help from civilians who live nearby. Many of the homes in Gettysburg were turned into hospitals after the battle.

What if I'm Wounded?

On the third day of the battle at Gettysburg, you are wounded and find yourself in a field hospital, which is just a large tent set up for doctors and surgeons. You are lucky that your wound is not serious—just a cut on your arm from some exploding shrapnel. Eventually one of the nurses comes to clean and bandage your wound. You are able to return to your company in a few days. While you are at the field hospital, you learn how terrible the conditions are. One of the biggest problems is that doctors do not understand how germs cause disease—there are no antiseptics or antibiotics. Many wounds become infected, and thousands of men die from these infections. For this reason, any serious wound in an arm or leg means it is amputated!

DISEASE. More deaths are caused by disease than by battlefield injuries. Thousands die of the measles and the mumps, as well as typhoid, malaria, and dysentery.

SAWBONES. Many surgeons have had no formal medical training and are only skilled at pulling teeth and amputating limbs. Surgeons are called "sawbones" by the soldiers.

A FEMALE DOCTOR. Mary Walker was the only woman doctor to serve in either army in the Civil War. Dr. Walker was a surgeon and served with distinction. She was the first woman to be awarded the Congressional Medal of Honor.

Handy Hint

If you do make it to a real hospital, you will be treated by trained nurses. There were 3,200 nurses serving the Union army, and about 9,000 civilian volunteers.

This won't hurt a bit.

What About the Navy?

FIGHTING IN THE NAVY.
All sailors are issued weapons and trained in their use, but there is very little hand-to-hand fighting between ships' crews in battle.

When you have time, you write to your cousin who enlisted in the Union navy. According to him the Union navy had 42 ships at the beginning of the war. One of the Navy's strategies was to blockade all Southern ports, but to control the huge coastline the number of ships had to be increased. By the end of the war there are 671 fighting ships, making the U.S. Navy the largest in the world.

thud

" ...lucky to be on a ship, as we don't have to march everywhere like you do and I think that the food we get is probably better than what you describe... "

24

In one letter, your cousin describes the most famous naval battle of the war. Most ships in the 1860s were made of wood, but the Union *Monitor* and the Confederate *Merrimack* (also known as the C.S.S. *Virginia*) were different— they were ironclads. In March 1862, the two ships engaged in a three-hour battle. Each took at least two dozen direct hits, but the cannon balls bounced off the iron plating. Neither ship sustained serious damage. The battle ended because the crews were so exhausted they could not load the cannons anymore.

Handy Hint

It is much safer in the navy. Of the 100,000 men who serve in the Union navy, only about 200 are killed and less than 200 are wounded.

25

1864 – Total War

In early 1864, General Grant is appointed commander of the Army of the Potomac. In May, he begins a series of battles against Lee that slowly pushes the Confederate army backward to Richmond and then beyond to the railroad center of Petersburg, Virginia. For several weeks, your unit is marching, fighting, and marching again. You don't get any time to rest or write letters and many nights you don't get any sleep at all. Some of the fighting is the worst you have experienced in the war. At Petersburg, the Confederates dig trenches and set up strong earthworks which are too well-defended to attack. For the next few months your unit is camped outside Petersburg. The war is a stalemate, with the Union army slowly starving out the Confederates in a siege.

ULYSSES S. GRANT. Grant (left) becomes the most successful Union general. When the war started, he was working in his brother's store in Ohio— by the end of the war he is one of the most famous generals of all time. Grant becomes so popular that he is elected president in 1868 and 1872.

Handy Hint

Siege warfare is tedious. The effect on morale is as important as the lack of food or supplies. It is also boring for the army that is laying siege. Keep your spirits up!

Forward!

BOOM

A BIG BANG. Union miners dug a 500-foot (150-m) tunnel under the Confederates and loaded it with four tons of gunpowder. The explosion created a crater 170 feet (50 m) long, 60 ft (18 m) wide, and 30 feet (9 m) deep. Union troops tried to attack through the crater, but the Confederates regrouped and drove them back.

How Does It All End?

THE END OF THE LINE. In his retreat, Lee was trying to join forces with another Confederate army in North Carolina. When he realized he was surrounded, he was forced to surrender.

After ten months, the Union army forces General Lee's soldiers out of Petersburg. Your regiment is part of the advancing army chasing the Confederates along the Appomattox River. You are in several small battles, but the Confederates keep retreating. Lee's army is finally trapped near the village of Appomattox, Virginia. On April 9, 1865, you hear a rumor that the Confederates are going to give up. Your unit is given the honor of guarding General Grant during the surrender. You put on your best uniform and march to Appomattox. General Grant and General Lee meet in the home of Wilmer McLean to discuss terms, and in less than an hour the surrender agreement is signed. The war is over!

In 1861, Wilmer McLean was living near Manassas, Virginia. His house was used by Confederate generals as a command post during the first battle. Some people say the war began and ended in Mr. McLean's living room.

THE WAR IS OVER! In American cities, church bells ring out in celebration. After four years of fighting, you can finally go home to your family farm in Connecticut.

If you are a Confederate soldier, you can keep your guns, horses, and mules. Most men in the South were farmers and General Grant allowed them to leave with the things that would be useful when they returned to normal lives.

HandyHint

I'll be hunting with this!

It looks much better on you.

29

Glossary

Amputation Having a part of your body, particularly a limb, cut off by a surgeon.

Artillery Units of soldiers that transport and fire cannons in battle.

Blockade To prevent ships from entering or leaving a port.

Canteen A water bottle.

Carbine A lightweight rifle with a short barrel.

Cartridge box A leather box that holds ammunition for a rifle.

Casualty A person who is wounded, missing, killed, or captured in battle.

Cavalry Soldiers who fight on horseback.

Company A military unit of about 100 men. Ten companies make a regiment.

Deploy To position soldiers for a battle or for defensive purposes.

Earthworks Walls of earth and logs which soldiers build for protection.

Enlist To join the army.

Field hospital A temporary hospital set up near a battle to care for the wounded.

Grits Broken grains of corn that are used in many recipes in the southern United States.

Hardtack A hard biscuit or bread made with only flour and water.

Infantry Soldiers who fight on foot.

Insignia A badge of office, rank, or membership.

Ironclad A ship with iron plating on the outside.

Malnutrition Not having enough good food to maintain one's health.

Morale The general level of confidence and happiness.

Musket A long-barreled muzzle-loading gun used by the Confederate infantry.

Private The lowest ranking enlisted soldier in the army.

Regiment A military unit of about 1,000 men.

Reinforcements Additional soldiers who are added to help in a battle.

Secede To leave an organization or nation to form one that is independent.

Sergeant Soldier who is in charge of a company.

Shrapnel Fragments from an exploded artillery shell, mine, or bomb.

Siege Surrounding an army and waiting for them to surrender.

Uniform Clothing that soldiers wear that are the same for everyone.

Important Battles of the Civil War

The Battle of Bull Run
(also known as the Battle of Manassas)
July 21, 1861

The Battle of Hampton Roads
(CSS *Merrimack* vs. USS *Monitor*)
March 9, 1862

The Seven Days
June 26 – July 2, 1862

The Battle of Antietam
(also known as the Battle of Sharpsburg)
September 17, 1862

The Siege of Vicksburg
May 18 – July 4, 1863

The Battle of Gettysburg
July 1 – 3, 1863

The Siege of Petersburg
June 15, 1864 – April 2, 1865

Index

Women at War

Women were not officially allowed to serve as soldiers during the Civil War, but some exceptionally courageous women found a way around that. They led a double life—either by spying or by disguising themselves as men so they could fight.

Harriet Tubman was an escaped slave who worked as a nurse and a spy. She led an armed raid on the Combahee River in South Carolina and freed more than 700 slaves. She persuaded many more to leave their enslavers and join the Union army. She hoped that if the Union states won the war, slavery would be abolished. (She was right.)

Sarah Emma Edmonds fought for the Union disguised as Private Frank Thompson. She spied on the enemy, nursed the wounded, and carried mail.

Mary Edwards Walker was one of the first women in the United States to graduate from medical school, in 1855. The army did not allow her to be a surgeon, so she served as a nurse. Eventually, in September 1863, she became the first female U.S. Army surgeon.

Frank

Sarah

Did You Know?

- At the Battle of Antietam in September 1862, nurse Clara Barton felt her sleeve "flutter." Looking down, she found that the soldier she was helping was dead. A bullet had passed through her sleeve and into his chest.
- Barton was called the Angel of the Battlefields. In 1881, at age 60, she founded the American Red Cross, which she led for the next 23 years.

Top Ten Bloodiest Battles

1. **Battle of Gettysburg, Pennsylvania (July 1–3, 1863)** This battle resulted in 51,000 casualties, of whom 28,000 were Confederate soldiers. The Union was considered the winner of the battle. Later that year, on November 19, 1863, President Lincoln attended the dedication of the Soldiers' National Cemetery in Gettysburg. His speech was short (269 words!) and lasted only two minutes. Not much was thought of the speech at the time, but today it is considered one of the greatest speeches ever given.

2. **Battle of Chickamauga, Georgia (September 19 and 20, 1863)** While the Confederates won this battle, the price was high—as in many of the Civil War battles. Killed, wounded, and missing Confederates amounted to 18,000 of the 66,000 soldiers engaged. Union casualties were 16,000 of the 58,000 involved.

3. **Battle of Spotsylvania Court House, Virginia (May 8–21, 1864)** There were 30,000 casualties, of which 18,000 were Union soldiers. There was no clear victory for either side.

4. **Battle of the Wilderness, Virginia (May 5–7, 1864)** It resulted in heavy casualties for both sides (29,800), but the battle had no clear winner.

5. **Battle of Chancellorsville**, **Virginia (May 1–4, 1863)** In this significant victory for the Confederates, there were 14,000 Union casualties and 10,000 Confederate casualties.

6. **Battle of Shiloh, Tennessee (April 6–7, 1862)** About 23,746 men died, of which 13,047 were Union soldiers. There were more Union than Confederate casualties, but the battle prevented the Confederates' advance.

Did You Know?

- Lots of soldiers were homesick for their families. The only way they could contact each other was by writing. Each day, 90,000 letters passed through Washington, D.C. Soldiers used lead pencils because pens and ink were rare.